This

BUZZABLE™
BABY BOOK

Belongs To

Buzzable Baby Book
Stacey Valle and Gina Stock

Copyright © 2012 Buzzable, LLC
Published by Buzzable, LLC
Phoenix, Arizona
www.BeBuzzable.com

Notice of rights
All rights reserved. No part of this book may be reproduced or transmitted in any form or by any means, electronic, mechanical, photocopying, recording, or otherwise, without the prior written permission of the publisher.

For information on obtaining permission for reprints and excerpts, please contact hello@bebuzzable.com.

Notice of liability
The information in this book is distributed on an "as is" basis, without warranty. While every precaution has been taken in the preparation of this book, neither the authors nor Buzzable, LLC shall have any liability to be caused directly or indirectly by the information contained in this book.

Some graphic elements used within this book were obtained at vectorstock.com.

Printed in Canada by
Friesens

ISBN 978-0-9857913-9-1

A sincere thanks to our wonderful friends and family who always support our new ideas.

Introduction

Right now the Buzz is about you and your new baby! Get showered with tips and sweet sentiments from those you know and trust. Ask your family and friends to join in the fun by filling your pages with parenting wisdom. You can easily refer to their helpful tips and cherish their sentiments anytime along your parenting journey. One day you can pass your book on to your own child and continue the BUZZABLE BABY BOOK tradition.

Table of contents

Welcome Home Baby — 11
Preparing for your new arrival

Hungry Bellies — 19
Success at feeding time

Nite Nite Baby — 27
Getting your sleepyhead to bed

Baby on the Move — 35
Wiggling, crawling, standing…

Infant Essentials — 43
Things you just can't live without

Chompers — 51
Tiny teeth, BIG pain

All Aboard — 59
Traveling with baby near and far

Daddy Says — 67
Wise words from dads who know

Mommy Time — 75
Finding Balance

Resources — 83
Where to find help

How To

Use this book at your baby shower as an activity to bring guests together. Here are examples of the types of entries you will find in this book. Feel free to follow the examples provided or get creative and add your own personal touch.

When you see a box...

fill it with a helpful tip
OR
a funny story

xoxo: Sign & date

Tip From: Name & Date

Share your best tip or home remedy.

Lists

When there's a list feel free to add away!

In your own words

Draw a picture or write a sweet message.

Sign it with Love!

Heavy markers are not recommended

Welcome Home Baby
Preparing for your new arrival

Welcome Home Baby
Preparing for your new arrival

Tip from:

Tip from:

Tip from: _BUZZABLE_

It's so much fun to make the nursery a place where baby and parents can enjoy spending time. Before baby comes home, make a special room filled with love.

Tip from:

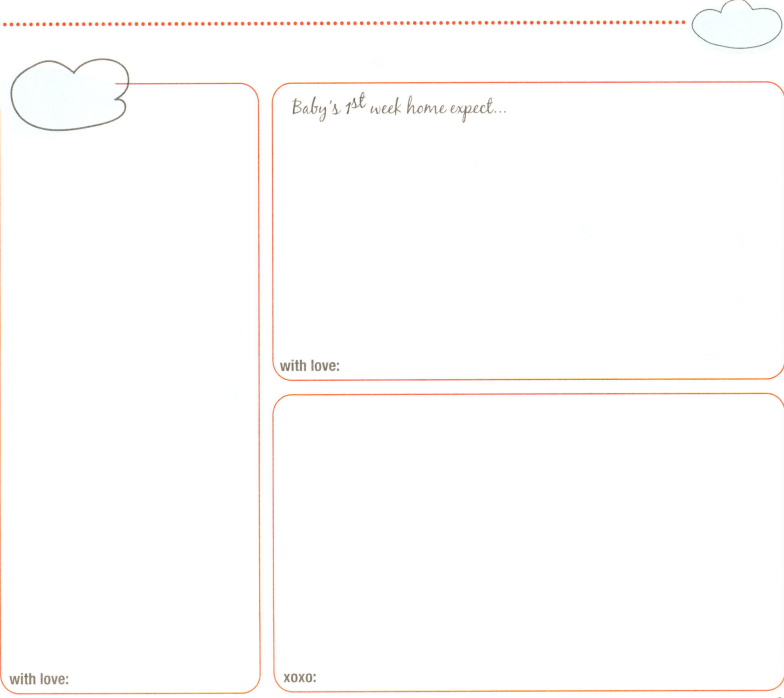

Baby's 1st week home expect...

with love:

with love:

xoxo:

Welcome Home Baby
Preparing for your new arrival

In your own words…

Hungry Bellies
Success at feeding time

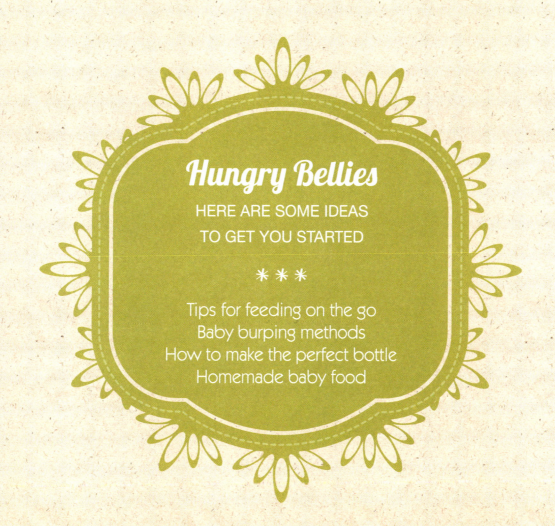

Hungry Bellies

HERE ARE SOME IDEAS
TO GET YOU STARTED

✶ ✶ ✶

Tips for feeding on the go
Baby burping methods
How to make the perfect bottle
Homemade baby food

Hungry Bellies
Success at feeding time

Tip from: _____

Tip from: _____

Tip from: _____

Before baby arrives check out different methods for feeding time. Remember, you won't know what will work until baby is born. Try not to worry, you'll be a natural before you know it.

Tip from: _____

with love:

with love:

xoxo:

Hungry Bellies
Success at feeding time

In your own words...

Nite Nite Baby
Getting your sleepyhead to bed

Nite Nite Baby

HERE ARE SOME IDEAS
TO GET YOU STARTED

✳ ✳ ✳

Tips for sleeping through the night
Bedtime rituals
Taking turns getting up
How to avoid bad habits at bedtime

Nite Nite Baby
Getting your sleepyhead to bed

Tip from:

Tip from:

BUZZABLE

Tip from:

It can be helpful to set a routine of activities before bed. Pick a spot that you use each night for winding down so baby will know bedtime is near.

Tip from:

If baby can't sleep try...

xoxo:

xoxo:

with love:

Nite Nite Baby
Getting your sleepyhead to bed

In your own words...

Baby on the Move
Wiggling, crawling, standing & falling

Baby on the Move

HERE ARE SOME IDEAS
TO GET YOU STARTED

✳ ✳ ✳

Tips for baby proofing
Pets and your baby
Clearing the way
Keeping up

Baby on the Move
Wiggling, crawling, standing & falling

Tip from:

Tip from:

Tip from:

Research the best methods for securing heavy furniture. As baby starts to move, you will want to prevent large items from being tipped accidentally.

Tip from:

with love:

with love:

xoxo:

Baby on the Move
Wiggling, crawling, standing & falling

In your own words...

Infant Essentials
Things you just can't live without

Infant Essentials

HERE ARE SOME IDEAS
TO GET YOU STARTED

✸✸✸

Tips on where to find the best stuff
Cool toys and gadgets
Items for outings
Music, movies, and books for baby

Infant Essentials
Things you just can't live without

Gadgets

Toys

Miscellaneous

Learn infant CPR

Lotions + Potions

Kitchen Must Haves

xoxo:

xoxo:

xoxo:

with love:

Infant Essentials
Things you just can't live without

In your own words...

Organization is Essential!
Put frequently used items together in a cute basket and keep one in each room where the items are needed. This can save time in your daily routine.

BUZZABLE

Chompers
Tiny teeth, BIG pain

Chompers

HERE ARE SOME IDEAS
TO GET YOU STARTED

✳ ✳ ✳

Tips on making baby comfy
Old remedies
Teething phases
Anything that will help

Chompers
Tiny teeth, BIG pain

Tip from:

Tip from:

BUZZABLE

Tip from:

Make sure you know when to expect teeth. You may have to try a variety of things to make your little one comfy during this difficult time.

Tip from:

You know they're teething when…

with love:

with love:

Soothe sore gums with…

xoxo:

Chompers
Tiny teeth, BIG pain

All Aboard
Traveling with baby near and far

All Aboard

HERE ARE SOME IDEAS
TO GET YOU STARTED

✻ ✻ ✻

Tips for packing
Entertaining baby
Airport anxiety
Takeoffs and landings

All Aboard
Traveling with baby near and far

Tip from: _____

Tip from: _____

Tip from: __BUZZABLE_____

Always have a travel bag filled with essentials. If you restock it after each outing, you can quickly walk out the door knowing you're ready for just about anything.

Tip from: _____

with love:

with love:

xoxo:

All Aboard
Traveling with baby near and far

In your own words...

Daddy Says
Wise words from dads who know

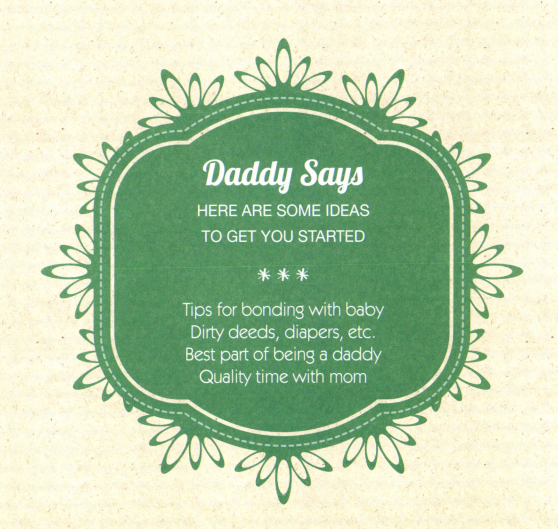

Daddy Says

HERE ARE SOME IDEAS
TO GET YOU STARTED

✳ ✳ ✳

Tips for bonding with baby
Dirty deeds, diapers, etc.
Best part of being a daddy
Quality time with mom

Daddy Says
Wise words from dads who know

Tip from:

Tip from:

BUZZABLE

Tip from:

Work out a transition plan with your partner. Remember you both may need a few minutes to unwind from the day. Be proactive and plan for this transition together.

Tip from:

xoxo:

xoxo:

with love:

Daddy Says
Wise words from dads who know

In your own words…

Mommy Time
Finding balance

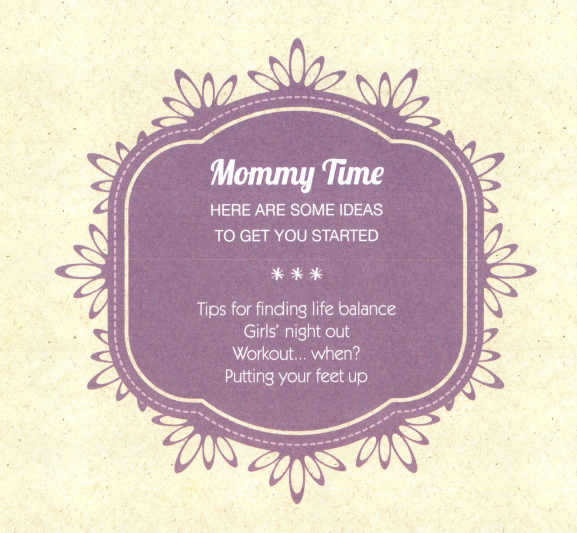

Mommy Time

HERE ARE SOME IDEAS
TO GET YOU STARTED

✳ ✳ ✳

Tips for finding life balance
Girls' night out
Workout... when?
Putting your feet up

Mommy Time
Finding balance

Tip from:

Tip from:

Tip from: BUZZABLE

Consider hiring a babysitter so you can run errands or have some one-on-one time with a friend. Making time for yourself is important so you can be refreshed with lots of love and joy to share.

Tip from:

Mommy Time
Finding balance

In your own words…

Resources
Where to find help

Resources

HERE ARE SOME IDEAS
TO GET YOU STARTED

✳✳✳

Tips on when to ask for help
How to find a good doctor
When to expect walking, talking, etc.
Favorite baby stores or websites

Resources
Where to find help

Wonderful Books

Great Websites

What Doctors Do I Need

Favorite Baby Stores

Parenting Blogs

Where to Find Sitters & Daycare

For great advice turn to...

xoxo:

xoxo:

with love:

Resources
Where to find help

In your own words...

To Baby
Special wishes for baby

We hope you enjoy your Buzzable Baby Book and wish you a lifetime of happy parenting.

With love,

Stacey & Gina